Caged Fugitive

Troy Lovell

Trapped but running. Losing and finding. Caged: not free .Lost. Broken. Different. A poetic rendition of life on an emotional roller coaster

Contents

See me.

The best things
I have to say
Are tantamount to
No words.
Nothing. Even if I try, will form into sentences.
Only chopped
Words with nothing to do with each other
So I'm silent.
Not shy silent.
It's really loudly screaming at you behind one of those sound
proof glasses begging you to listen and to hear the yelling and to
open the window so my thoughts can run on like this sentence.
A caged bird has nothing on this song that I'm singing, because
everyone is listening to her and loving her, but not hearing me.
It's not fair
Life's not fair. But i complain
Because I like to.
She's just trapped behind bars, she can't fly. But I can't talk.
If you listen to my silence you might hear everything
But then you might finally see me
And I'm afraid of that
Because I can open the window myself if I wanted to.

Soul created

I am HER
She is the side that reflects
All that I want to be. But cant.
Because I am not.
The victim
Created in a story, that isn't real
With a lifestyle that didn't happen
Because she does not exist
But it feels that way

Because her creator
Believed in every detail
Of her being
Molded her personality
Better than a snow in August.

Storyteller

Had to make up a
Symbol with a name
One who would shoulder
Blame
For leaving me.
When I'm the leaver.

A story to make me
Feel better
About being scared
(Conniving)
Of commitment
And locks
Where I can't swim

Afraid to be stuck in loose sand
By chains.
So I leave before the metal hardens.
Before the worst
After the best is started and feels done with
I leave.
And weave
Fairytales of something perfect leaving me
Causing me pain.
When I'm the leaver
Who was thought perfect

Causing pain

But inflicting freedom on myself.
And ending care easily
Just making stories to make me the victim.
when
I'm the victimizer.
The leaver.
The story teller

Bare

Wondering if I'm the only one
who's feeling like
everyone around them
is staying the same
while they're changing.
Changing real fast.
so fast that those people
quickly blurr away
and become
boring
annoying
immature
and a part of your past?
and then you're left feeling
all alone
until you find new people
who you hope won't fall in the prior cycle?

kind of in that, all alone sentence
just waiting for someone who can stay.
changing the same exact
pace that I change.

Smile

frown

cry

close the curtain

laugh

smile

to someone

at someone

sit

act like you care

ignore your problems

press repeat:

keep laughing; keep smiling

wake again

press repeat:

frown

cry

close the curtain

behind a wall

behind your shield

behind your conscience

fake it.

laugh

smile.

Lie

Defamation
Can slide over my lips
Like butter for body
Over skin
And I hate.
That I can't stop
Because it feels low, so low.
And sometimes I want to
Be down there.
Deep down
Where I feel I belong. But
Deep where I'm not allowed to be.
Because no one lets me
So lies
Where they don't belong
Succumb
To make me feel
Like the equivalent of how I want to be seen.

But I don't want to be seen
How I think people see me.
Just something worse.
I get more than I deserve
Why?
Do I not want good things? I can't accept it

Except
I pick the wrong
Un truths

Begin to cover me
And create new seen imagery
Envisioned by me.
And I want to stop
But I can't
I'm telling
the truth
Is what I need.
I need to stop.
Talking. I want to.
To hide.
Lie to hide
Real
That I'm afraid,
And now I cant
Lie.

Train

You must not know
How horrible it is to form joints
Inside of bones.
The pain and the agony.

I hate saying agony.

I still lose my thought looking in your eyes.
But in a bad way.
I used to want to know
What you were thinking.
Now I want to know how your pupils got so ugly.

Is it because your soul is disgusting?
Or because you justified why I think,
I might want to hate humans

You asked to learn me.
Why would you ask me that.
What can you learn about me,
If you forgot that I have a temper.

Dumb questions...

Does this side of the platform go uptown?

Please go downtown.
If you walked a mile in my shoes, your feet would melt.

If you walked a mile beside me.
I'd shoot
Save you the trouble,
Of being a traveling whore.

All the girls you like will come see you.

What I don't like is how you seemed to get so tired.
So quickly.
You have
Ugly
Downtown eyes.

Burning lust

Sensation
In the palm of my hand
Deep in there
Wishing she was not testing me right now
Every rude remark making
Me want to shake
Her.

I'm trying

She's pushing
Every single thing that reads...
"please do not fucking push me"
She is making my blood burn
She wants it charred
Dark red burning
Because she won't stop
Her self restraint

My self restraint
Is melting
Touching her hair in a hall
Wanted to grab it
So that I could place my mouth on her neck
And bite deeply.
Fucking audiences
Ruin scenes
Ruin moments
And my actions

I need her to stop talking to me because
I'm pleasured
Without
Touch
And she's still talking.
She wants me to grab her
I can't stop looking at her
Because I want to touch

Lustfully ranting
I'm ranting
And I can't do that.
The next time she tells me to shut up I want to
Grab her jaw
And bleed her lips with my teeth
Grab her waist
And rip into her hips

So she tells me to stop
But I won't
Because it's her fault.

That I'm growing impatient
Growing lust.
And hating that damn lollipop
I pulled it
But I should've
Pushed it down her throat
Making her choke
Would be the death of me.

Or actually cutting her and rubbing
The dripping blood.

Robbing me of my self control
Eyes closed in class
Toes curled in boots.
For no reason,
Just words.
Fingers gripping pen
Because I can't grip her.

My palms are still burning
Wishing my chest wasn't so heavy
And since she's making my inner thighs weak
I feel like digging into hers.

Wishing she didn't keep
Catching me looking at her.
I used to be good at that.
Wish I wasn't looking
Wish I could stop.
Few words
Few face
Expressions

Are consuming me

Running from apparent sexuality.
Wish my palms were not still burning.

Deep lip scars

In front of me

I'll stare

At the spot on

Her neck

Where my lips belong.

My teeth belong.

Gently

Entrenched

In her seat.

Lay her down

Softly

Not

Tearing her apart.

Yet.

Just smooth

Shy movements

Like brushing fingers over her body

To drive me

Her wild

Sweet almost moans.

Deep lips scars

Then

Sweet full moans

Nails into skin:

I want them loud

Hands stealing her breathing

Wanting her louder

Becoming the lightening

Sparks between her thighs

Wanting to set her

On quiet fire

Hands over her mouth

Silent screams

Smothering my fingers.

Tongue along

The. Spot on her neck where my lips belong.

Fear.

Always trying
Always failing
At being unafraid.
fear becomes
Different
A feeling so good
Radiating off of me.
So scared to touch you the wrong way.

Hands entwined
With your fingers
My fingers on you
Feeling so right
So wrong.
Wanting you
So sweet.
You under
My exploring hands
So sweet.

My lips against your skin
So soft
So hot
Raising goosebumps
Creating goosebumps
So wrong so right.

Afraid to cross
A boundary

To cross the line.
Your lips
So nice against mine.
Laying there
So beautiful
No need to touch me back
All I,
Want.
Need is
To touch you.
To hold you.

Power growing
With your flesh under my nails
Your shivers
pushing back against my hands
Body rocking
Neck throbbing
Under my lips.
I stop.

Not wanting to cause too much
I break a lot that I touch.
Afraid
Afraid
Afraid
But you shudder
And you look so beautiful
Weak.

That I want to
Hold you
Have you
For myself
Hold you
Hear you
Breath

Listen
Smell you
Just stay there, for days.

And I am afraid.

Move through Me

I'm
The embodiment of fear
That I may have
May be
In love
I feel myself
Trying to run
While stuck in one place
While lost.
And confused about
How I'm running and staying in the same spot?
Because a female is making me forget my pain
The pain I was having
Is changing
Into a she.

So scary
It is so scary
That I listen to music
And have visions of me touching her
I breath and a daydream about breathing her.
I taste how cold air is in winter
And think about how warm she would taste
And I'm scared.
That I want to listen to her
Talk about everything
When I stopped caring

About words
Other's words
And hers are now drugs.
I'm addicted,
And I know
Because it hurts when she walks away from me.
And my heart chokes when I can't see her
Feel her
Presence.
Watching her talk and move
Gave me chills
I wanted her.
And having her touch and move
Through me.
I need her.
Scared to need.
Scared because this became accidentally on purpose.
That this is the best I feel
Felt in the longest.
And I don't
I can't feel good.
I don't deserve to.
Need her.
Terrified.
But not to have her.
Terrified just to have,
Fear of potential
Faults.
Terrified of love.

Why did you come here?

Trying to hide my.

Trying to hide behind

Trying to conceal
My composure.
Always
Tired
Of trying.
In the end being
Haunted by the things I
Tried to ignore: You, and her now, him
Trying to
Now
Because I grow cold
Quickly
On everyone.
Trying not to leave
Anyone.
Leave her
Or him
Hanging.
But
That is my response to pain
Ignoring it
Letting it slip from under my skin
To under yours.
Not giving a fuck
How bad you hurt.
Because that's how bad I felt
Still feeling it.

So harsh.
So I tell you
Its ok
And
I'm not mad
And
No you're not.
When I really
Want to stop replying.

Because, seems like when I open up
I break.
I can't get more broken.
So I can't be open.
I'm closed.

You will always be a huge part of me
One
Non-lie
I told in the past tense
Of two minutes ago.
Because I will never forget
You.
Almost
Caused me re-pain.
I was closing and
You came and re-opened me
Left the wound drenched in blood
Why would you
Re-open it
Infect it.
I thought you would make it better
But I'm back open. To my past
Left to mend this all alone again.
I am nothing.
But I guess that
Happens
When you try to eat salad
With a spoon.
Shit like that doesn't
Work.
don't rush
But can't wait
Won't wait
Because I don't want it.
I am nothing.
Speaks of.

Means speaks of.
But what does not speaking mean
Knowing
And I don't.
You had the nerve to
Come here.
And I let you in
You were scared
And I take liking to weird
And I should not take liking.
Now I'm here
My heart is upset with me
For nurturing everything but it.
And I smile. About to smile. Backwards.
Why did you come here?

What I'm scared of

I tell

people all the things I'm afraid of

and my list is

always scant.

I'll say clowns. Knowing that that isn't my real fear

I'm just extremely disgusted by them

So they're less scary than repulsive.

I'll bat a lash

to change the subject.

Ask me

and I'll confidently say

"nothing"

I'm not afraid of anything.

The conviction of the sentence

the non-shake in the back tone of my

always shaky wordless voice

will tell you that I am telling the truth.

But I perfected that lie.

She is afraid of one thing.

Afraid that

she isn't afraid of anything, but swallowed undigested time.

Jigsaw

We form the bottom

 edges of a jigsaw .

Our raw edges are not a match

we do not fit

the complete opposite.

But we put the two straight edges against each other

and tried to make it work

our raw edges facing two different ways.

for a while we stayed

together; ignoring the obvious that we were made, but not for each other

because when the puzzle needed to be completed

worked on

we couldn't figure out how to interlock our sides to form a union

and we ended up having to separate and

find the part of the puzzle

where we belonged.

Even though we did

and still do not

want to.

Find AWAY

What does Keys know about
Broken hearts?
Finding a way
Is not easy
When you can't find away.
Holding tight
It's impossible to let go
To loosen
Up.
So stop it
You can't skip around pain.

I tried too much
Too many times.
And learned that
Teary eyes
Raging
Chest pain
Stomach aches
And headaches
Are your armor.
Armor needed
Because you need to run through it
Right through it.
You have too.
Running around the sprinkler
Does not get you wet
And that's the only point
When you are hot
It is hot.
And I'm living in the feeling
Because there is no way
To not be lonely after
Annihilating closure.
Finding away is impossible
So running becomes possibility.
My reality.
Finding a way
I run from
And into
Everything.
A chronic runaway
From lies
And pain before it gets here,
And pain that is already here.
Try sleeping?
Sleep been dead.
I need to be in your bed
You holding me

Once more,
For me to finally give in.
Sleep does not exist
With pain
Insomnia consumes.
Finding away
Finding
A way
You crumple
I am crumbling
Always falling.
Never making it
Always running.
Find
Which
Way?

Question

Why
Do I
Do this to myself?
Implications on things
Reminding me of you
I force you into my brain
Into me
When I'm almost done forgetting you.
Because I don't want to.
Mentally
Emotionally screwing myself'
Worse than how you
Mentally
Emotionally
Screwed me.
Why ?
Cause I shouldn't care about who's new to you

Or if you don't feel right with anybody else but me
Like me.
I just wonder when would
I be
Able to cross you
Come across you
Your name
Any implicate
Intricate
Aspect of you.
And be madly in love with someone else
So it wouldn't
even
Phase me

Feel Good Hurt

Burying some thing harder sharper than pain.
Shoveled deep under my personality. So it can't swallow me
Erupts after a few moons that are orange, like volcano back wash.
Takes over all cells moving, and air passages not breathing.
Clogged but melting away
By strict strikes of matches.
Too cold to run, in shoes with points competing with ice.
I lay. Lay in bed, eyes blinded by piercing stares of ceiling gazes,
and red patterns.
I lay, and dig into myself. Until. The outer fire blasts off, showing
off that she's now way more intense than the inner.
She wins. The mind focused on the colors and the burn of the
outside. And now I can
Feel good and sleep.

The Wall

First thing I
See
Signing on is her
Her name.
And the words love.
Is more than one word
Its three
Infatuation is two
And I'm one of those
Why once I loosen up
Do I get dumped
Thrown off of a cliff
Suicidal homicide
Because I'm putting my own wrist out
For others to cut.
And it hurts.
That I have to be two people.
An exterior and an interior
Everyone always seeing the latter
Because when I show the first
I get hurt.
So perfectly vulnerable
To everything
When breaking that wall protecting me.
Smile is my wall.
Wall
Takes forever to come down
And
Quickly re-builds.
Lost a few bricks when I came down twice
So I feel like people will be able to
Dig their hands in the holes.
And the
First things they'll see are
Two names.

Blood,
Froze over
Cold
Pain.

Unfold Me.

I am screaming

The blood cells, flowing through. every vein and ventricle

Are curling bubbling boiling

With rage.

Boiling with rage and fear.

Crying, moaning, shouting,

Till my fists are bald tightly.

Fist balled tightly because I'd like to punch something; and I'm trying not to grab my hair out but I need something to grasp.

Everything is folding into itself.

Cells folding into veins, folding into ventricles, collapsing my heart.

My heart is collapsing, smashing.

It already crashed and smashed, the raging blood is flying freely, flowing depressingly through my body.

Shocking me.

Melancholy

I am trying not to be depressed.

But it is flowing threw me.

Folding me.

I am waiting.

For you to arrive

And please unfold me please.

No one is going to come along and twist me, tug me, wrap me, hold me.

Like you did.

My pride won't let me tell you, that I need you.

I try.

I swear I try to act like I was not affected by my leaving you.

But I am.

At night my mind is vulnerable to the 1000 feelings of everything collapsing.

Getting rid of you, is adjacent to taking the backbone out of a human.

And I want you, to yell at me.

It turned me on.

But you're not here.

So I'm looking for someone to yell at me.

And ask me about my day, too many times in the same day.

Send me smiley faces for no reason.

And kisses for all reasons,

Deemed right.

You held my hand too tight when I said something you didn't like.

So I'm looking for that.

Looking for someone to tell me they love me, and they need me, and they want me.

Like you did.

Wanting someone to tell me that I'm pretty, and I smell good, and I taste good.

I taste good... I want them to repeat it a million times like you did. I got tired of listening to you say that. But I'd do anything to hear those words come out of your lips or any lips.

I want somebody to wait for my knees to shake, and wait for me to shake, and drink my aura, and take off with me

I want you to do it.

They cannot do this.

Who are they.

There is no one.

To grab my hair

And grab my neck

And scratch me up.

To an extent where I forget about all the pain surrounding me. Because the digging and the pulling. You are the pain.

You are not here

You are the pain.

Searching for an alternative

Because I'm not the girl who

Scrapes her knees begging, because I'm the girl who's pride consumes her.

The girl that boards trains at 2am

Searching for answers, and new feelings, and new places.

Because maybe there is someone new in Huntington New York.

There aint shit in Huntington New York.

I was there

And you wasn't

So I lighted a damn bench

And boarded the train.

Not knowing that I'm looking for you. But knowing that you are who I am looking for.

Light a bench

Board a train

Head home

To my spot in the window, where I sit and watch soul-less people walk by

I watch but I can't see them

Because I'm gone off

Wondering.

Why I can't find you

Why are you not walking by?

Why are my tears so red?

And why I can't see anything

I can't see anything.

Ever.

It's been a fucking year and I can't get over how I can't get over you.

I can't escape from your pathetic no good ass, because I'm just as pathetic and ten times more no good.

I always give my shit away, then regret it.

I gave you away and can't get you back because you are gone.

So I'm waiting for one person that will really make me forget you because I fucking hate you.

Someone who will never let me think about you,

salt water out of tear ducts for you.

I'm tired of burning my eyes, burning my brain, burning benches burning my throat, my nose my mind because of you.

Constantly running out of lighter fluid.

From fucking burning.

Tired of running away

Even though I love it.

Running away in every way

From ranting, to writing, to running, feels so

It feels good to escape. Everyday.

It is a drug; escaping is.

I'm running to everyone that reminds me of you, and running away from them for the same reason.

Running to everyone opposite you, and running away from them for the same reason.

I really hate you.

Please unfold me.

I want to take the shocks off.

And stop running.

Stop running from love, before it touches me.

Because

after,

it touched me.

Please unfold me please.

Broken

Leave me the alone
Leave me alone
Leave me.
Screaming so loudly on the inside
I'm screaming
Can't you hear?!!
No one can hear me
You can't hear me
Anymore
I'm not here.
I wish I was here
You hearing me.
I hate this song
I hate songs
Especially this one.
I remember the orgasm
That you gave me

In the climax.
first orgasm
We became one
with each other.
And then we split.
I'm still holding on.
I want to let go but I don't
Because hating you feels so good.
I hate you.
I hate you for moving on
Forgetting about me
I am not here.
I swear I'm not.
And every time the beat drops
I remember the shiver
And nobody but you has been able to make me feel this way.
You broke me.
I'm broken.
Broken.
Took away all the good parts of me
So the people that come
And put me together
Cant.
I am
Manufactured
One small twist and I'm done.
You took all my bolts,
Of electricity
They are still in your body
I feel them
Through you.
The beat fucking dropped again.
And I have this song on repeat because
It is the only thing that makes you real.
Real tears come, and I know that
Though deleted
You are still

Here in my bed
Where I need you.
I hate you because it feels good to do so.
And you promised.
And you made me feel like nothing mattered
And then you lied to me.
I hate you
Get out of me.
I want you here
don't leave me.
don't scare
Me.
I'm scared because you lied to me.
Left me floating
Left me drowning.
And I can swim

But I'm letting myself drown
Because the pain is so bad it feels good.
And I hate you.
I will never be real for anyone
Because you stole me. And I still feel you
Wanting to feel me
Through everybody that tries to take me.
But they can't take me
Because I am nothing.
I don't work
And I want you to feel my pain
But I feel stupid.
For still wanting you.
It's been a whole year.
And I'm afraid
Please
Leave me alone.
Go away.
Stay.

Signs

"Aquarians are often very attached to the first real commitment in their lives and they can even re-marry a previously divorced partner."

My problem:
I'm attached to my first
and I see the million cons
but refuse to unlight the few pros
I've had way better
but it never feels right.
It was so wrong
all very.
I refuse to acknowledge your significance when I'm alone
But my subconscious vomits you
and you
find your way in becoming the main idea
of my ruined relationships.
You know when to come back, and peek through the cracks in a surface.
And I wish I could have loved something better first.
Because now I have a hard time repeating
So I may never be in real love again.
I won't be.
I acquired paranoia
and my body's defenses are strong
fighting against the "what ifs" that may occur
after the infatuation passes.
when there may be only lust left.
First love
I hope no one ever finds a boy like you
But I hope they do.
You
left me immune to
feeling.

Left me in transformation from
Distressed tension,
To blankness
I have a hard time repeating
So I'm thinking, maybe I'm not supposed to.
Maybe he ruined it for me.

I am blank.
Upset that I'd take you back in a heartbeat,
When I don't even remember
How to have one
My first love left me organ-less
Empty.

Blank